WOMEN IMPRESSIONISTS

To Rasaad Jamie

First published in the United States of America in 1986 by
Rizzoli International Publications, Inc.
597 Fifth Avenue, New York, N.Y. 10017

Second Impression 1987

Copyright © Phaidon Press Limited, Oxford, 1986

Library of Congress Catalog Card Number: 86-42733
ISBN 0-8478-0757-6 (pbk.)

Printed in Great Britain by Blantyre Printing and Binding Company Limited, Glasgow

Eva Gonzalès: *Morning Awakening* (detail of Plate 18)

WOMEN
IMPRESSIONISTS

TAMAR GARB

RIZZOLI
NEW YORK

1. Henri Fantin-Latour. *Studio in the Batignolles Quarter*. 1870. Oil on canvas, 68½ × 82 in. (173 × 208 cm.) Musée d'Orsay, Galerie du Jeu de Paume, Paris

Few people will have heard of the women Impressionists. While paintings and histories of paintings have ensured that the reputations of Edouard Manet, Auguste Renoir, Alfred Sisley, Camille Pissarro and Claude Monet have all survived, the names and works of Berthe Morisot, Marie Bracquemond, Eva Gonzalès and Mary Cassatt are far less well known. Even in those pictures that document the relationships between the artists and writers who challenged academic painting methods from the late 1860s until the 1880s the female presence appears only in the guise of muse, model or art-historical reference. Henri Fantin-Latour's *Studio in the Batignolles Quarter* (Fig. 1), 1870, which portrays Manet, Monet, Renoir, Bazille, Zola and Astruc, does not include a woman artist in the group, despite the fact that Morisot and Gonzalès were both part of the Manet circle; on the other hand, a statuette of a female figure is placed conspicuously on the table. The unspoken message is clear. Women in the nineteenth century were deemed more appropriate as the subjects and inspirations of art than the creators of it.

Who then were these women artists who belonged to the group of French nineteenth-century independent painters, known as the Impressionists? What was their relationship to this group, to their male colleagues and to other women artists of their time? How were they viewed by their contemporaries? And how is it that art history has so eclipsed their contribution?

It is misleading to create, in retrospect, a common identity for four very different artists that is based on the fact of their sex. Each of the women Impressionists related in her own specific way to the artistic and political debates of her time. The four painters did not consciously identify themselves with each other, and the strongest intellectual and aesthetic collaborations that they developed were with their male colleagues rather than among themselves; important were Gonzalès's and Morisot's relationships with Manet, Cassatt's with Degas, and Bracquemond's respect for Monet's contribution to art. Friendship and professional consideration existed between Cassatt and Morisot, and Gonzalès and Morisot knew one another. Bracquemond seems to have had less contact with the others. Cassatt, of all the women Impressionists, was the most politicized about her femininity and consequently established strong ties with women artists, primarily, though, outside the Impressionist circle. This belies the popular assumption that the Impressionists were a close-knit and exclusive group, completely separate from their more conservative contemporaries.

Here were, then, four painters who were deeply engaged in the artistic debates of their time. They can no more be identified as a group simply by their femininity than can the male Impressionists be exclusively explained by the constraints of their masculinity. Nevertheless, the conditions under which these women artists worked and lived were different from those of their male colleagues and, to a certain extent, their social and psychological situation accounts for the work they produced.

The institutional restraints on becoming a professional woman artist in the late nineteenth century were numerous. There was no free state education for women in fine art, and the official state art school, the École des Beaux-Arts, was only opened to women in 1897 after a protracted struggle by women artists. Women were hampered by their general education since the curriculum for girls differed markedly from that of boys. A classical education, deemed essential for success in the fine arts, was not available to most women. Only those whose private tutors regarded such study as suitable, or individuals of exceptional ability and drive, like the artist Marie Bashkirt- seff, would have been schooled in that range of material from which much of the subject matter of art was drawn. It was their lack of general education and academic training, their domestic situation and their social and psychic conditioning that led many women to concentrate on small- scale genre painting and still life throughout the nineteenth century. The critic Paul Mantz in 1865 praised Berthe Morisot's submission to the Salon while satirizing the genre in which she worked: 'Since it is not necessary to have had a long training in draughtsmanship in the Academy in order to paint a copper pot, a candlestick, and a bunch of radishes, women succeed quite well in this type of domestic painting.' The belief that women were incapable of handling complex subjects led teachers to restrict the range they offered them. In 1860, Marie Bracquemond wrote of Ingres: 'The severity of Meur Ingres frightened me . . . because he doubted the courage and perseverance of a woman in the field of painting . . . He would assign to them only the painting of flowers, of fruits, of still lifes, portraits and genre scenes.'

Most wealthy women artists trained at private academies like the Académie Julian, which were expensive, or at studios organized by artists like the society-painter Charles Chaplin, who ran an all-women life class and accepted women as private pupils. Both Gonzalès and Cassatt were his students. Nearly all women who were serious about becoming artists enlisted as copyists in the Louvre. It was here that Bracquemond first met her artist husband, Felix, that Morisot first noticed Manet, and that Degas situated his series of etchings of Mary Cassatt (Fig. 2).

Even more inhibiting than the meagre practical provisions for the training of women artists was the pervasive pressure on bourgeois women to regard art as a necessary accomplishment rather than as a professional commitment. This was accompanied by the belief that it was unlady- like to excel in art since women's true talents centred on home making and mothering. One contemporary commentator, Octave Uzanne, claimed that 'if a woman chooses to occupy her leisure time in trying to reproduce beauty . . . what does it matter whether she has talent or not? . . . many women possess quite enough of it to please their husbands, educate their children in good taste, and beautify their homes.'

Often, women who engaged seriously in artistic or intellectual pursuits were considered 'masculine', and it was widely believed that these tasks were unsuited to them by nature. While dabbling in art was suitably feminine, excelling in it was regarded as subversive and even

2. Edgar Degas. *Mary Cassatt at the Louvre*. 1879–80. Etching, $14\frac{1}{2} \times 10\frac{1}{2}$ in. (36.3 × 26.6 cm.) The Cleveland Museum of Art, Cleveland, Ohio

dangerous. It was in this context that the painter Guichard, the Morisot sisters' first teacher, warned their mother: 'Considering the character of your daughters, my teaching will not endow them with minor drawing-room accomplishments, they will become painters. Do you realize what this means? In the upper class milieu to which you belong, this will be revolutionary, I might almost say catastrophic.'

Despite the pressures on women not to become professional artists, unprecedented numbers of them did so in the Paris of the Third Republic. The network of artists' societies and exhibiting forums in Paris provided a diverse context in which women's art could flourish. While some of these societies were exclusively female institutions, such as the *Union des Femmes Artistes*, with its annual *Salon des Femmes*, others were mixed group shows, such as the exhibitions of the *Independants* organized in the 1870s and 1880s and dubbed 'Impressionist'. Morisot was instrumental in the organization of the Impressionist exhibitions, but Gonzalès never showed her work in them, preferring, like her mentor Manet, to exhibit at the Salon. Cassatt was politically committed to the idea of exhibitions where the paintings were not selected by juries. When she was invited by Degas to exhibit with the Impressionists in 1878, she accepted with joy: 'At last I could work with complete independence without concerning myself with the eventual judgement of a jury.' Marie Bracquemond exhibited at the Impressionist exhibitions of 1879, 1880 and 1886.

Although much has been made of the homogeneity of the Impressionists' aims, the diversity of practices within the group is obvious. What unites them is their common intention to evolve

3. Louise Abbema. *Luncheon in the Conservatory*. 1877. Oil on canvas, 76 × 121 in. (194 × 308 cm.) Pau, Musée des Beaux Arts

a painting technique distinguished from academic painting, with its high degree of surface finish, its subtle gradations of studio lighting and grandiose historical content. The Impressionists, in differing degrees, committed themselves to the search for a pictorial equivalent to visual experience and to contemporary subjects. They rejected photographic realism, exemplified by the works of artists like Louise Abbema (Fig. 3), and sought to find ways of approximating, through textured surfaces, asymmetrical compositions, broken brushstrokes and heightened colour, the active sensations of vision itself. While Morisot, like Monet, Bracquemond and Sisley, can be seen to have explored the transitory quality of light and its effects on colour and atmosphere, Cassatt, like Degas and Gonzalès, was more concerned with drawing and compositional structure, and with achieving a quality of monumentality and permanence.

Of all the women Impressionists, Marie Quiveron Bracquemond is the least known. She, unlike Cassatt, Morisot and Gonzalès, did not come from a prosperous, cultured milieu. As a young woman, she was admitted to Ingres' studio, where she gained the reputation of being one of his most intelligent pupils. Her marriage to Felix Bracquemond in 1869 introduced her to her husband's circle, which enabled her to make important artistic contacts. Ironically, the marriage also inhibited her development as an artist. Felix Bracquemond was one of the foremost engravers of the time, but, although he taught his wife etching, she produced only nine etchings (Fig. 4). In an etching of his wife and her sister, of 1876, Felix shows Marie drawing on the terrace of their home at Sèvres (Fig. 6). In the late 1870s, influenced by Monet and Renoir, and to her husband's dismay, Bracquemond became interested in *plein-air* painting; her colours intensified, and she became increasingly committed to the Impressionist aesthetic of rendering contemporary events in unmodulated colour and painterly brushmarks. Felix Bracquemond became a firm opponent of Impressionist methods. He believed that tone, value and composition should be carefully worked out before the final painting was executed. Marie Bracquemond, on the other hand, was a fervent defender of Impressionism to the end of her life. 'Impressionism has produced . . . not only a new, but a very useful way of looking at things. It is as though all at once a window opens and the sun and air enter your house in torrents,' she declared when Felix attacked what he termed the 'folly' of painting out-of-doors.

From 1880 onwards, her painting subjects were consistently of contemporary life, but it is unlikely that she would have executed a drawing like *The Umbrellas* (Fig. 5) on the spot. Although many women, including those who exhibited at the Salon like Marie Bashkirtseff, depicted aspects of contemporary urban life, their paintings were usually executed in the studio. Bashkirtseff expressed her frustration at the restrictions placed on women artists: 'What I long for is the freedom of going about alone, of coming and going, of sitting in the seats of the Tuileries, and especially in the Luxembourg, of stopping and looking at the artistic shops, of entering churches and museums, of walking about the old streets at night; that's what I long for; and that's the freedom without which one cannot become a real artist.' Felix's disapproval of his wife's painting methods, his jealousy of her talent and his inability to take her criticism, made

4. Marie Bracquemond. *Woman at Easel. c.* 1890. Etching, 12⅜ × 9⅞ in. (31.5 × 25 cm.) Paris, Bibliothèque Nationale

5. Marie Bracquemond.
The Umbrellas. 1882.
Charcoal and white paint
on paper, 10 × 15 in.
(25 × 38 cm.) Louvre,
Cabinet des Dessins,
Paris

6. Felix Bracquemond.
*The Terrace of the Villa
Brancas.* 1876. Etching,
10 × 13⅞ in. (25.5 × 35.5
cm.) British Museum,
London

the atmosphere at home unbearable. Worn down by lack of recognition and continual domestic friction, she abandoned painting in 1890, executing thereafter only a few small works.

Berthe Morisot's domestic situation could not have been further removed from Bracquemond's. She was already a mature painter when she married Eugène Manet, brother of Edouard Manet, in 1874. She had, in her husband, a man who offered unqualified support for her endeavour as an artist and complete sympathy and understanding for her approach to painting. Remembered most often in the history books as Manet's beautiful model (Fig. 7), she was, herself, one of the moving spirits behind Impressionism, instrumental in formulating its aesthetic, and faithful to the idea of organizing and exhibiting in independent exhibitions.

Morisot, the youngest daughter of an upper-middle-class family, was born in Bourges in 1841. Her first teacher, Guichard, disapproved of her and her sister Edma's wish to paint out-of-doors, and they soon left him to work with the celebrated landscapist Corot and his pupil Oudinot. In 1868 Morisot was formally introduced to Manet, whose work she admired enormously, but he was never her teacher. Indeed, the relationship was far more reciprocal than is generally assumed, and Morisot was instrumental in urging Manet to work *en plein air* in the 1870s and 1880s. She showed her paintings from the first exhibition, of 1874, to the last, of 1886, missing only that of 1879 after the birth of her daughter. Morisot was, in fact, regarded by critics as a quintessential Impressionist. In 1877 Paul Mantz wrote: 'There is only one impressionist in the whole revolutionary group—and that is Mlle Morisot . . . Here it is truly the impression felt through a sincere eye and faithfully recorded by a hand which does not cheat.'

Although she did not exhibit with the Impressionists, Eva Gonzalès was closely involved in the movement towards naturalism and realism. She shared with the Impressionists an interest in the depiction of modern life themes and evolved a technique of broad and painterly brushmarks, which reveal her debt to her teacher, Manet. She is better known as the model for Manet's portrait than for her own work, and many accounts of her life dwell almost equally on her personal beauty and on her talent as an artist. Indeed Manet's portrait of her (Fig 8), elaborately dressed and daubing at a flower still-life, can be read as the classic image of the accomplished female amateur. Gonzalès produced a substantial body of work in her short life (she died at the age of 34 in 1883); at her retrospective organized by her husband, the artist Henri Guérard, and father, Emmanual Gonzalès, in 1885, eighty-five works were shown.

Of the four women Impressionists, it is Mary Cassatt whose work is most widely reproduced and often discussed. An American, born in Pittsburgh in 1844, she trained at the Pennsylvania Academy of Fine Arts and settled in Europe after extensive trips there to study art. When she first exhibited with the Impressionists in 1879, she was thirty-five years old and had already shown in the Paris Salon and other major exhibitions for more than ten years. She had been strongly attracted to realism from early on, and became committed to an art that represented modern life. Although Cassatt is best known for her paintings of mothers and children, most of her works are portraits and figure compositions. (Having executed her first *maternité* painting

7. Edouard Manet. *The Rest, Portrait of Berthe Morisot.* 1870. Oil on canvas, 61 × 44½ in. (155 × 114 cm.) Museum of Art, Rhode Island School of Design

8. Edouard Manet. *Portrait of Eva Gonzalès*. 1970. Oil on canvas, 78¾ × 53⅛ in. (201 × 135 cm.) National Gallery, London

in 1880, she only began to concentrate on this theme in the 1890s, when she and many Symbolist painters made it a popular subject.) During her Impressionist years in the late 1870s and early 1880s her range of subjects was wide. She became increasingly interested in Impressionist technique, even though she, like Degas, was concerned with drawing and combined a taut pictorial design with the evocation of optical experience.

It has been common for critics, writing about women artists, to praise a few, while generally denigrating women's endeavours in art. When the novelist and critic J. K. Huysmans admired Cassatt's images of children he found the reason for their excellence lay in Cassatt's femininity rather than in her skill as an artist. 'Woman alone is capable of painting childhood . . . only the woman can pose the child, dress it, pin it without pricking it', were his words of praise for this highly intellectual woman, who, in fact, had no children herself. Huysmans compares Cassatt's talents with those of other women artists, who, he fears, turn 'to affectation or to tears'. The Irish novelist and critic George Moore similarly put down all other women painters in his praise for Morisot. Her pictures, he wrote 'are the only pictures painted by a woman that could not be destroyed without creating a blank, a hiatus in the history of art'. As recently as 1982, Jean Dominique Rey praised Morisot's work for not falling into the 'trap of excessive muscularity or falsely masculine toughness' of Cassatt or of Suzanne Valadon slightly later.

While Huysmans's praise for Cassatt rested on her successful handling of what was, to him, an appropriately feminine subject, Morisot is often lauded for painting in a suitably feminine style. Her touch is repeatedly described as delicate, graceful and charming. It was this that George Moore so admired, claiming that 'she has created a style, and has done so by investing her art with all her femininity; her art is no dull parody of ours: it is all womenhood.' Teodor de Wyzewa wrote in 1891 that the Impressionist method was one most suitable to bring forth a feminine painting, in that its bright tonality was appropriate for the lightness of character and the superficial elegance that constituted a woman's vision. Roger Marx, in 1907, declared that the term 'impressionism' itself implied a manner of perceiving and recording which corresponded well to the hypersensitivity and nervousness of women.

Such attempts to explain the achievements of the women Impressionists undermine the seriousness of their endeavours and posit the notion of an essential, unchanging femininity. The assumption that an innate propensity towards delicacy or superficiality accounted for the way the women Impressionists painted disregards their commitment to the aesthetic that the group—of men and women—to which they belonged, consciously evolved. What is more, it ignores the fact that the majority of women painting in the late nineteenth century were not Impressionists but represented the whole gamut of artistic production. In order to be fully understood, the work of the women Impressionists has to be considered in the context of the important aesthetic and political debates of their time. It is through an examination of these debates, together with our appreciation of the situation in which they, as women artists, worked, that we can realize the extent of their achievements.

1

BERTHE MORISOT

Catching Butterflies (1873)

Oil on canvas
18 × 22 in. (46 × 56 cm.)
Musée d'Orsay, Galerie du Jeu de
Paume, Paris

Morisot spent the summers of 1872, 1873 and 1874 with her sister's family at Mourecourt. It was here that she executed *plein-air* scenes in paint and pastel, usually depicting a woman and one or more children (her nieces) in a garden. The year 1873 was the last in which Morisot showed at the Salon, and by 1874, when *Catching Butterflies* was shown at the first Impressionist exhibition, she was committed to a painting technique that, through the use of light grounds and the direct application of brushmarks, strove to approximate the fleeting sensations of vision itself. The palette of her early teacher, Corot, with its variety of grey, green and brown tonalities, continued to influence Morisot in the early 1870s, her surfaces soon became increasingly painterly, with a variety of brushmark and notation, which was shared by her Impressionist contemporaries. In *Catching Butterflies*, the grass, trees and foliage are described in fluid but controlled strokes, and the apparent freedom of application of paint is belied by a carefully considered compositional structure. It was the apparent lack of finish and sketchiness of the application of paint that critics denounced. Guichard, the academic teacher whom Morisot had left in order to enter Corot's studio, gave the following advice after seeing the exhibition: 'She is to go to the Louvre twice a week, stand before Correggio for three hours, and ask his forgiveness for having attempted to say in oil what can only be said in watercolour.'

2
BERTHE MORISOT

Summer's Day (1879)

Oil on canvas
18 × 29½ in. (46 × 75 cm.)
National Gallery, London

Summer's Day, first shown at the Impressionist exhibition of 1880, is one of the first of Morisot's paintings of the Bois de Boulogne, which became one of her favourite motifs in subsequent years. The Bois was still a sylvan retreat in the late nineteenth century and was a popular spot for promenaders and picnickers. Morisot sought out secluded spots, and concentrated on capturing the reflections in the lake, the lush vegetation, and on creating an image of an idyllic harmony between figures and their surroundings. The poet Paul Valéry described her relationship to the forest:

> Living on the edge of the Bois, she found it gave her landscape enough: trees, the gleaming lake, and sometimes ice for skaters. She was often teased by Mallarmé, a lyric enthusiast for the trees of Fontainebleau, on account of this taste she had for the moderate groves and the mediocre shades that are all that is to be had between the Porte Dauphine and the Seine. For him, the Bois was a meagre affair, devoid of mystery and lofty groves. But Berthe contented herself with nature's Parisian parsimony, taking from it what it gave, the themes for some exquisite works.

The Bois provided Morisot with the setting for a variety of subjects. Not far from her home, it was easily accessible and suitably sedate for a woman artist, her child and female models, to inhabit.

For *Summer's Day* Morisot used professional models. She executed first a watercolour sketch and then the oil painting. Morisot had worked in watercolour from the 1860s and became increasingly interested in the immediacy and atmospheric effects that this medium offered. By 1879 she had evolved a technique that attempted to retain this liveliness in oils; she used broad brushstrokes and pale grounds to indicate the movement of light over the surfaces of landscape and figures.

3
MARY CASSATT

Woman and Child Driving
(*c.* 1879)

Oil on canvas
35 × 51½ in. (89.6 × 130.8 cm.)
Philadelphia Museum of Art
(The W. P. Wilstach Collection)

Cassatt was primarily a figure painter. Where landscapes appear in her works they are used as settings, most often a secluded and enclosing garden, occasionally the more open spaces of lake or forest. *Woman and Child Driving* has as its setting the Bois de Boulogne, which on weekends was transformed from the quiet park used by the residents of Passy, like Morisot, as an extended garden, to a fashionable gathering place where Parisians would go for walks or drive about in horse-drawn carriages. The horse and carriage portrayed here were the newly purchased possessions of the Cassatt family, bought after Alexander Cassatt had established a trust fund for his parents which significantly augmented their income. Pictured driving the new carriage is Lydia Cassatt, the artist's sister; accompanying her is Odile Fèrve, Degas' niece. A young groom is seated at the back. The focus of the painting is the two female models. The groom's face forms a silhouette against the dark forest, which conveys little of his personality or character. In contrast, the faces of Lydia and Odile are carefully delineated. The woman concentrates intently on her task, her face composed and serious, while the child's head tilts slightly forward, her downward gaze indicating that she is deep in thought.

Cassatt does not capture the motion of the moving carriage. Her asymmetrical composition and cropping of edges serves to concentrate our attention on the two female figures, one a serious young woman, the other a pensive child, so that what can be read initially as a genre painting becomes instead a double portrait. For Cassatt it is the psychological presence of her female sitters that is crucial. And, in this case, the male figure acts as a foil to the object of her study, the mature active woman and the dreamy child.

4

EVA GONZALÈS

The Donkey Ride (c. 1880)

Oil on canvas
32 × 39½ in. (81.5 × 100 cm.)
City of Bristol Museum and Art Gallery

The models for Gonzalès's modern life paintings were drawn from her close family circle. Her sister Jeanne, clothed in blue, is seated on the donkey while Henri Guérard, Eva's husband, casually leans on it with his gaze fixed attentively at her. The conventional placing of the figures and the donkey, and the careful breaking up of the surface at the golden section, indicate Gonzalès's familiarity with traditional pictorial arrangements. The eyes of the man are fixed on the woman, who, situated at the centre of a conventional triangular arrangement of forms, directs her languid gaze outside the canvas, towards the viewer. The psychological ambiguities that such an interaction of 'looks' sets up recall the many canvases by Manet in which a straightforward narrative reading is impossible.

The handling of the surface, and the picture in being relatively unfinished, offer an important insight into the painting procedures that Gonzalès inherited from Manet, her teacher. Manet had learnt from Couture to work his *ébauche* (sketchy underpainting) evenly over the entire surface. Gonzalès uses dilute, transparent oil washes, loosely brushed in; she leaves many areas of the beige support bare, or reveals the thin, animated brushed lines that indicate the position of the figures. While certain areas, like the donkey's head, are highly finished in deft and confident painterly marks, areas like Guérard's body are barely suggested by the brush. Nevertheless, the colours of the painting when complete are already clearly indicated: the subdued grey, green and blue tonalities are relieved by the scarlet cherries gleaming on the straw hat and the touches of red on the donkey's coat.

5

EVA GONZALÈS

Reading in the Forest (c. 1880)

Oil on canvas
42 × 54 in. (106.5 × 137 cm.)
Rose Art Museum, Brandeis University,
Waltham, Mass.

It is often a tamed and inhabited nature that Impressionist imagery presents. While Morisot, Bracquemond and Monet often explored the effects of sunlight on flesh and fabric in reassuringly domestic outdoor spaces, Gonzalès's rendering of figures in the open air resisted the current tendency to break up form into a film of light and incandescent colour. Even Manet had, by the 1870s, lightened his palette and experimented with Impressionist techniques of dissolving form in light. Gonzalès's figures, though, retain their solidity, the contours remain firm and the subtle interaction of greys, greens and neutral tones so characteristic of her palette are ever present.

Although the role of 'spontaneous', 'on the spot' painting has been much exaggerated (and with it the belief that the Impressionists responded intuitively to an objective outside world by recording their immediate sensations of it), it is true that much painting done by the Independent artists, at least in the 1870s, was done *en plein air*. That the artists engaged in a process of recording, adapting and reworking is now widely acknowledged, and the links of Impressionist methods with traditional planning and composing are accepted. Gonzalès's paintings of outdoor scenes rarely attempt even to achieve an effect of spontaneity, nor does her brushwork and range of colour aim at approximating the processes of vision. In *Reading in the Forest* she is clearly a traditionalist in the careful placing of the figures, in the filling of the empty lower right-hand corner with the hat and crook, and in the positioning of the dog as an anchoring mechanism for the figure on the left. These figures were obviously drawn in the studio and the completed painting is a carefully composed study, which is rooted in the realist and naturalist tendencies of Courbet and Corot.

6

MARIE BRACQUEMOND

Tea Time (1880)

Oil on canvas
32 × 24 in. (81.5 × 61.5 cm.)
Musée du Petit Palais, Paris

The subject of figures in a garden was popular with many of the Impressionists, most notably Monet, Renoir, Cassatt, Morisot and Bracquemond. For the women it offered an opportunity to explore the possibilities of *plein-air* painting without having to venture far from home. It is the sitter's mood of intelligent absorption that differentiates the portrayal of female models by the women Impressionists from so many of the works of their male colleagues. While Renoir detested models who thought, Pissarro evoked a mythic image of the natural peasant, and Monet only occasionally focused on the psychological presence of his sitters, the women Impressionists presented images of women resonant with dignity and self-containment. It was to Monet and Renoir, though, that Bracquemond turned for her understanding of Impressionist technique. In a later discussion between Marie, Felix and his student, Gaston La Touche, Marie Bracquemond puts up a heated defence of Renoir and Monet. Of the latter she declared: 'No one has ever arrived at a power of analysis of tonal values at once so intense and so sweet . . . I cannot say at what point Monet arouses my emotion, but he produces in me such sensations as make me happy, but which I would not have discovered by myself. He opens my eyes and makes me see better.'

It is Bracquemond's new interest in faithfully recording the effect of brilliant sunlight that is so clearly evident in *Tea Time*. The quiet domestic scene, so typical of bourgeois suburban life as portrayed by the artists of the Third Republic, is illuminated by an all-over glow, which allows figure, still life and background to merge through colour. Patches of colour recur over the surface, the pinks of the bonnet, face, dress and still-life objects are repeated in the highlighting of the trees, and the fragmented brushstrokes right across the canvas create a surface that seems to vibrate with reflected light and colour.

7

BERTHE MORISOT

Young Woman Sewing in a Garden
(1884)

Oil on canvas
$23\frac{1}{4} \times 28\frac{1}{2}$ in. (59 × 72 cm.)
National Galleries of Scotland,
Edinburgh

Morisot painted scenes of women and children in gardens throughout the 1870s and 1880s, and more and more preferred to render the enclosed spaces of the garden than the more panoramic landscapes of her earlier years. From 1882 to 1884 she worked often in the garden at Bougival where she, her husband and daughter, Julie, spent part of the year. They rented a house surrounded by a large garden at 4 rue de la Princesse. From the early 1880s Julie, born in 1879, was to become Morisot's favourite model, and it was through painting that she recorded the growth and development of her only child. The image evoked in *Young Woman Sewing in a Garden* is one of tranquil domesticity, with woman and child each engaged in a task of her own. Julie watches her sailing boat in the shallow pond while the woman, probably a nurse, is absorbed in her needlework. Like Cassatt, Morisot did a number of works showing women sewing. Embroidery and needlework were widely regarded as a naturally feminine pastime in the nineteenth century, and girls were taught to sew from an early age. Embroidery was thought not only to signify femininity but to be instrumental in inculcating suitably feminine behaviour.

The placing of the sewing woman in a tranquil domestic landscape, which includes a child, situates her firmly within an accepted setting for a nineteenth-century woman. But Morisot avoids the overt moralizing that contemporary *maternité* paintings betrayed. Indeed there seems to be a barrier between the two people, provided by the tree cutting the centre of the surface vertically. Each of the models seems fixed within her own psychological space. There is no attempt to represent an idealized relationship appropriately staged. Instead, the effect created is of a moment observed.

8
MARIE BRACQUEMOND

The Artist's Son and Sister in the Garden at Sèvres (*c.* 1890)

Oil on canvas
21½ × 18 in (55 × 46 cm)
Private collection

Marie Bracquemond's son Pierre and her sister were her staunchest supporters. It is to Pierre that we owe the detailed documentation of her life in his unpublished manuscript, 'La vie de Felix et Marie Bracquemond'. It is he who records the pain and difficulties which his mother suffered because of the conflicting demands of her responsibilities as wife and her needs as an artist. He records, too, his father's jealousy of his mother's talent and his inability to accept her criticism. It was for these reasons that Felix Bracquemond rarely showed his wife's work to the artists who frequently visited their home. It was Pierre who arranged the retrospective in which 156 of Marie Bracquemond's works were shown at the Galerie Bernheim Jeune in 1919, three years after her death.

This painting was one of the last works by the artist, executed over twenty-five years before her death. The setting is the garden of the family home to which Maria Bracquemond confined herself for most of her adult life. In later years she rarely visited people and almost never went to exhibitions or galleries in Paris. In this double portait, Pierre, now twenty years old, is formally posed next to his seated aunt, his mother's close companion. The features of the two models are carefully recorded through an analysis of the play of light on their faces. Bracquemond continues to seek colour in shadows. Her flesh tones are permeated with greens, greys and blues and the clothing of her models serves as a reflective surface for a wide spectrum of colours.

Bracquemond continued to defend the Impressionist way of working until the end of her life. Even after she stopped painting, when she lived a solitary and secluded life at Sèvres, she vocally supported the principles which had informed her work in the decade 1880–90.

9
MARY CASSATT

Lydia Crocheting in the Garden at Marly (1880)

Oil on canvas
26 × 37 in. (66 × 94 cm.)
The Metropolitan Museum of Art,
New York

Lydia Cassatt was one of her sister's favourite models. Shown reading, weaving, crocheting or sewing, in the family home or in a private garden, she embodies the image of an accomplished late-nineteenth-century lady. She was forced by her long illness to cultivate interests that were not too physically exhausting and she remained at home with her parents (now living in France with Mary Cassatt) until her death from Bright's Disease in 1882. She and her sister were close companions, and Lydia's enforced passivity made her the perfect model for her sister.

In the summer of 1880, Cassatt and her family stayed at Marly Le Roi near Paris. It was here that she executed two portraits of her sister in the garden. Degas, on seeing her work completed in that summer, wrote: 'The Cassatts have come back from Marly . . . What she did in the country looks very well in the studio light. It is much stronger and nobler than what she did last year.' *Lydia Crocheting in the Garden* was shown at the sixth Impressionist exhibition of 1881, where Cassatt's work was praised by Huysmans:

> Her exhibition is composed of children, interiors, gardens, and it is a miracle how in these subjects, so much cherished by the English, Miss Cassatt has known the way to escape from sentimentality on which most of them have foundered, in all their work written and painted . . . For the first time, thanks to Miss Cassatt, I have seen effigies of ravishing youngsters, quiet bourgeois scenes painted with a delicate and charming tenderness . . . It is a special indication of her talent that Miss Cassatt, who, I believe is an American, paints French women for us. But in houses so Parisian she puts the friendly smile of an 'at home'.

MARIE BRACQUEMOND

The Three Graces (1880)

Oil on canvas
54 × 35 in. (137 × 88 cm.)
Townhall of Chemillé, Maine-et-Loire

This painting marks an important stage in Bracquemond's artistic development. It was painted only two years after her ceramic panel of the *Muses of the Arts*, which was shown at the International Exhibition of 1878 and presented women as personifications of abstractions, grandly attired and set in imaginary exotic surroundings. In *The Three Graces* Bracquemond presents a celebration of modernity. Three women, clothed in meticulously observed contemporary costume, assume the traditional positions of the legendary Three Graces, while, because of their obvious modernity, by-passing the associations of the mythical subject. Since large-scale figure compositions, often mythological, religious or historical in content, were still regarded as the most worthy of the painting genres at the annual Salons, the Independent artists sought to confer a similar heroism on paintings of modern life. Bracquemond's strategic use of a well tried pictorial formula (which traditionally included semi-attired classicizing figures) as a basis for her celebration of contemporary life, points to her engagement in the debates of her time.

Pierre Bracquemond, the artist's son, claimed that it was *The Three Graces* that marked a new stage in her stylistic development. 'She dreamt of larger compositions and conceived of three modern Graces, for whom she made a very beautiful cartoon in charcoal; she also made very beautiful sketches, sparkling with an audacious yet delicate palette,' he wrote. In her preparations for her paintings, Bracquemond remained a traditionalist. Meticulous and detailed preparatory drawings were made.

The painting was greatly admired by the critic Gustave Geffroy, who bought it from the artist. In his catalogue entry to the 1919 Marie Bracquemond retrospective, he describes the women: 'They give the appearance of a dream, as if they hovered above material things in the lightness of air . . . Their dresses . . . [are] the colour of copper, the colour of the sun, the colour of time . . . These three women, these delicate goddesses from another epoch enjoy a moment of joy in the greenery of this garden under the blue sky.'

11

MARY CASSATT

Five O'Clock Tea (1880)

Oil on Canvas
$25\frac{1}{2} \times 36\frac{1}{2}$ in. (64.5 × 92.5 cm.)
Museum of Fine Arts (The Maria
Hopkins Fund), Boston

The interior of the Cassatts' Parisian home is shown in this painting of a discreet bourgeois ritual. Cassatt's sister Lydia, in brown, partakes of afternoon tea with a fashionably dressed friend. The imposing silver tea service and porcelain cup gleam on the table in an elegant room with striped wallpaper and impressive fireplace, above which hangs a grandly framed painting. *Five O'Clock Tea* was shown at the fifth Impressionist exhibition of 1880, where it was admired by the critic Huysmans. It was in his comments, published in *L'Art Moderne*, that Cassatt was first called, inaccurately, a pupil of Degas:

> It remains for me now, having arrived at the world of M. Degas which I saved for the end, to speak of the two lady painters of the group, Miss Cassatt and Madame Morizot [sic]. A pupil of Degas, Miss Cassatt is evidently also a pupil of English painters, for her excellent canvas, two women taking tea in an interior, reminds me of certain works shown in 1878 in the English section [he refers here to the International Exhibition of 1878]. Here is still the bourgeoisie, but it is no longer like that of M. Caillebotte; it is a world also at ease but more harmonious, more elegant. In spite of her personality, which is still not completely free, Miss Cassatt has nevertheless a curiosity, a special attraction, for a flutter of feminine nerves passes through her painting that is more poised, more peaceful, more capable than that of Mme Morizot, a pupil of Manet.

Huysmans seeks to explain Cassatt's achievements by attributing them to her femininity. This results in contradictory and inconsistent perceptions. The 'flutter of feminine nerves' seems incompatible with the 'peaceful' and 'capable' qualities that he mentions. Writing on women artists is dogged by such attempts at acknowledging women's talents but, simultaneously, circumscribing them within a limited notion of femininity.

MARIE BRACQUEMOND

Under The Lamp (1887)

Oil on canvas
$27\frac{1}{2} \times 44\frac{1}{2}$ in. (70 × 110 cm.)
Private collection, USA

The Impressionist painter Alfred Sisley and his wife were regular guests at the Bracquemond home, and it is they who are portrayed at their hosts' dinner table in *Under The Lamp*. Mme Sisley is placed, half turned, with her back to the viewer while her husband is partially obscured by the golden glow emanating from the lamp. The evening light, with its ample cast shadows, and the sparkling highlights on bottle and glass are confidently handled.

Many of the Impressionist painters used their artist friends and their families as models. Both Monet and Renoir had, in the 1860s, executed paintings of the Sisleys, and in the 1870s, Manet, Renoir and Monet painted a variety of portraits and *plein-air* figure compositions of their own intimate circle. Marie Bracquemond was the hostess to many of the social gatherings initiated by Felix, and through his wide-ranging contacts she came to know many of the important figures in the Independent art movement.

In *Under the Lamp* Bracquemond demonstrates her, by now, consummate skill in compositional arrangement and still-life painting. She also reveals her ability to succeed in painting an ambitious figure study in a way that takes account of contemporary concerns to render modern life through the exploration of light and colour.

For all that, this painting provoked the following patronizing comments when it was sold in June 1971:

An unexpected name was Marie Bracquemond . . . wife of the painter and excellent engraver, Felix Bracquemond, who was an amateur painter who used the technique she learned from the Impressionists and executed various portraits of her husband's friends which, as well as being pleasing, are of documentary value. For this reason the canvas of Alfred Sisley and his wife at dinner was forced up by an American from $4,556 to $12,380.

13

MARIE BRACQUEMOND

Interior of a Salon (c. 1890)

Watercolour
8½ × 18½ in. (21 × 47.5 cm.)
Musée du Louvre, Cabinet des Dessins,
Paris

This delicately handled watercolour depicts a living-room in the Bracquemond home. The atmosphere is idyllic, with the soft afternoon sun coming in from an invisible window on the right and bathing the interior with its warm glow and dappled reflections. The room is comfortably furnished, with casual armchairs, plants and *objets d'art*. On the back wall hangs the grandly framed portrait of Louise Quiveron, *The Lady in White* (Plate 26), an important transitional work in Bracquemond's development from academic to naturalist styles. The watercolour, painted a decade later, includes this work, now hazily sketched in and without the crispness of the original outline, as a powerful and imposing presence in the quiet suburban room. Louise, Marie Bracquemond's sister, is reputed to have been 'strong', 'opinionated' and impatient with Marie's submissiveness to her husband. It is interesting, therefore, that this subdued and peaceful interior is dominated by the image of a woman who was Bracquemond's closest ally and friend while also being a constant reminder of her vulnerability.

In 1890 the domestic conflict that her painting provoked resulted in Bracquemond giving up painting almost completely (except for a few watercolours and drawings). Throughout her married life, she had been a committed mother and homemaker and was constantly aware of the conflicts between these roles and her wish to be an artist. In *Interior of a Salon* therefore, we see the touching juxtaposition of an apparently conflict-free interior, bathed in gentle sunlight, with the painting of *Woman in White* operating as a pointer to the life of the artist. On one level it recalls a seminal work done at a time of optimism and change, on another it represents Louise, always critical of Bracquemond's readiness to give in to her husband's demands, and whose presence must have kept her in mind of ambitions not fulfilled.

14
EVA GONZALÈS

The Little Soldier (1870)

Oil on canvas
51 × 38½ in. (130 × 98 cm.)
Townhall of Villeneuve-sur-Lot,
Lot-et-Garonne

This formal composition of a young uniformed boy was Gonzalès's first submission to the Salon, where it was exhibited in 1870. The model for the painting was a twelve-year-old boy whom she and her sister Jeanne had sought in a nearby barracks. Degas had painted a version of this theme in the late 1850s, and Manet's *The Fifer* was still in his possession at the time that Gonzalès, having entered his studio as a pupil, was working on her military portrait. Although Gonzalès uses the characteristic front lighting and indefined background space associated with Manet, the figure is finely detailed and meticulously drawn, with a degree of characterization of the face that is far removed from Manet's bold and simplified treatment. Gonzalès appears in the Salon catalogue as a pupil of the decorative artist Charles Chaplin. This painting provides an important link between the technique of highly polished surfaces, detailed rendering of form and traditional tonal modelling associated with Chaplin and his studio, and Gonzalès's later methods influenced by Manet. It was precisely this change in technique that was commented upon by many of the critics who wrote about the work when it was first shown. While there was general praise for her two other submissions to the Salon, which complied with accepted taste for detail and finish, *The Little Soldier* provoked a negative response in some quarters. It was called 'flat' and was derided for the absence of 'half tones', a complaint often directed against Manet's work. The shadows were called 'harsh' and the face 'plaster-like'. Some of the sympathetic critics expressed their surprise that such strength was possible from a woman aged only twenty, and it was claimed that her talents far surpassed those of other women who usually showed at the Salon.

15
BERTHE MORISOT

Psyche (1876)

Oil on canvas
$25\frac{1}{2} \times 21\frac{1}{2}$ in. (65 × 54 cm.)
Thyssen-Bornemisza Collection,
Lugano, Switzerland

In the mid-1870s, Morisot became increasingly involved in the exploration of light and colour in her painting. Like Monet, Sisley and later Bracquemond, she was particularly interested in the effect of light on white and set up a number of compositions to explore this pictorial problem. The subjects of these paintings were often of women at their toilette or in front of mirrors, sometimes dressed in low-cut white petticoats to reveal neck and shoulders. The practice of representing women in front of mirrors was traditional and relates to the old theme of Vanity, where Venus or another symbolic female figure is shown studying her own reflection. It is interesting to note that for many nineteenth-century theorists, the 'toilette' was thought to be women's highest form of artistic expression.

For the Impressionists, because of their interest in the study of reflected light, the mirror became an important element in their compositions. The theme of the woman at her toilette was explored particularly by Manet, Degas and Morisot, and it was a useful subject in that it offered a realist pretext for the exploration of a traditional theme. Although presented as images of contemporary life, with faithful recordings of light and colour, these paintings, like those of the Impressionist nude, were reinterpretations of an old convention, devoid of narrative content but still retaining the elements of the old story, woman, mirror and reflection. The traditional projection of narcissism onto women remains subtly present in these images.

Gonzalès used pastel throughout her working life. Of the eighty-five works shown at the retrospective held in 1885, the year after her death, at least twenty-one were pastels. *Pink Morning* was shown at this exhibition under the title *La Nichée*.

In his comments on the exhibition, the critic Philippe Burty praised Gonzalès's use of pastel and linked her achievements with the portraiture of the early eighteenth-century Venetian pastellist, Rosalba Carriera. It was quite common for critics to seek female 'ancestors' for women artists and Rosalba Carriera's name is mentioned by critics in connection with Morisot too. Not since her work, wrote Burty of Gonzalès's pastels, had he seen anything lighter nor more gentle nor anything that so expressed the very essence of pastel. (An edition of the Paris journal kept by Carriera had been published in Paris in 1865.)

In *Pink Morning*, Gonzalès creates a smoothly blended surface of subtle and muted colour. The gentle grey of the background, floral patterning of chair and pinks of the dress provide none of the vibrant colour contrasts of Cassatt's pastel work of the late 1870s. Neither is the surface animated with small energetic strokes, as in much of Morisot's work, nor suffused with energy, as in Degas's pastels. Gonzalès's effect is soothing and subdued, but, on close examination, the use of blue shadowing on the white cloth, the greyish blue on the dress, the variety of hues on the hands and the brilliant colouring of the border of the mirror, all become evident. The languid stillness of the image, with the young woman (probably modelled by the artist's sister, Jeanne Gonzalès) gazing contemplatively at the puppies in the basket, is typical of the many interiors with women that Gonzalès executed. This mood of self-absorption and quiet resignation often characterizes her paintings.

17
MARY CASSATT

Girl Arranging her Hair (1886)

Oil on canvas
$29\frac{1}{2} \times 24\frac{1}{2}$ in. (75 × 62 cm.)
National Gallery of Art (Chester Dale
Collection), Washington, DC

Manet, Morisot, Gonzalès and Degas all explored the possibilities of the theme of women at their toilettes. It was widely thought to be natural and proper for women, particularly, to pay close attention to their physical appearance. Many images of women tending their person, cleaning their bodies, combing their hair or powdering their faces, emerge from this period.

Cassatt's painting, while fitting into this genre, is also a touching portrait of an adolescent girl. The story around the inception of this painting has become legendary. Achille Segard, Cassatt's first biographer, recounted that it resulted from an argument between Cassatt and Degas. Degas had apparently claimed that women did not have the capacity to judge style, whereupon Cassatt was provoked to challenge his prejudice by producing a painting that would conform to his notion of artistic style. When the painting was exhibited at the eighth Impressionist exhibition of 1886, Degas is reported to have exclaimed: 'What drawing, what style'. He exchanged a pastel for this painting, which remained in his collection until his death, when it was auctioned. At the time of the auction in 1917, Cassatt wrote to Mrs Havemayer:

> The Degas sale will be a sensation. I am glad that in the collection of pictures of other painters he owned I will figure honorably, in fact they thought the two, a painting and a pastel, were his at first . . . I said to J.D.R. [Joseph Durand Ruel] it would not sell so well, but he said otherwise. It was the one he [Degas] asked me for and gave me the nude in exchange.

It is not difficult to see why Degas admired this painting. In it Cassatt has explored the same awkward and ungainly movements that Degas so enjoyed capturing. Her composition is tightly structured, with strong linear elements describing the space. The figure is confidently drawn in a way that combines linearity with a degree of modelling, which is consistent with Degas's own techniques.

18
EVA GONZALÈS

Morning Awakening (1876)

Oil on canvas
$32\frac{1}{2} \times 40$ in. (81.5 × 100 cm.)
Kunsthalle, Bremen

Gonzalès's commitment to realism is evident in this painting in which she presents her favourite model, Jeanne Gonzalès, in a relaxed and apparently unselfconscious pose. (*Morning Awakening* is one of two versions of the same theme.) Gonzalès places herself as the invisible observer of this intimate scene, but none of the overt erotic connotations of the theme, so often emphasized by contemporary painters, is here explored. The model lies in a position that obscures much of her body rather than revealing it. The arm hides the breast and the figure is clothed. The effect created is one of an accurate recording of a seen moment. A commitment to such faithful representations of reality was regarded as an expression of 'sincerity' and integrity by Realists and sympathetic republican thinkers. Maria Deraismes, a contemporary republican activist and protagonist of women's rights, praised Gonzalès's commitment to realism, and called her hand powerful and her brushstrokes solid and energetic. Such vigour, she declared, contrary to received opinion, was not dependent on muscular strength (and therefore masculinity) but on individual will. Claude Roger Marx, a contemporary critic and author of the only monograph on Gonzalès, called *Morning Awakening* a 'symphony of whites'; he pointed out the sensitive handling of fabric of the linen and of the muslin curtains and praised the freshness of the flesh tints on arms and face. The composition, as always with Gonzalès, is traditional, with the conventional draped curtain on the right included to achieve a sense of space.

19

EVA GONZALÈS

The Milliner (c. 1877)

Gouache and pastel on canvas
$17\frac{1}{2} \times 14\frac{1}{2}$ in. (45 × 37 cm.)
The Art Institute of Chicago

Paintings of working-class women in characteristic poses or settings became popular in the Realist circles of the second half of the nineteenth century. Gonzalès used a daily cleaner as a model for her painting. Degas had, in 1876, exhibited his first rendering of this theme at the second Impressionist exhibition, and he took up this subject again only in 1882 and 1883 when he executed at least four pastels showing milliners and their clients. Gonzalès's painting was shown at the Cercle Volney in 1882 and it was shown again at the Salon of 1883. Gonzalès's *Milliner* differs from representations of the theme by Degas in that because the woman has been placed centrally in a shallow space and made, unambiguously, the focus of the painting, it operates as a portrait rather than a genre painting. In the latter the anonymity of the figures is assured by their presence as types. Degas's very adventurous compositional arrangements, the cutting of edges and unconventional viewpoints, often direct the viewer's attention away from the figures.

Claude Roger Marx praised the work highly and regarded Gonzalès's use of pastel (here more textured and freely applied than in *Pink Morning*) as the high point of her work. He declared that *The Milliner* was 'as subtle as a Vermeer, as precise as a Liotard [the Swiss pastellist], and as authoritative as a Degas'. Gonzalès's confident handling of pastel, which she combines with gouache in this canvas, differs markedly from her earlier more traditional smoothness of finish. The surface is here animated with deft diagonal strokes, creating a lively overall rhythm of marks.

20

BERTHE MORISOT

At the Ball (1875)

Oil on canvas
$24\frac{1}{2} \times 20\frac{1}{2}$ in. (62 × 52 cm.)
Musée Marmottan, Paris

Morisot, like Cassatt, Degas, Manet, Gonzalès and Renoir (in the 1870s) was committed to the Baudelairean concept of representing the 'heroism of modern life'. For Morisot this included the activities of her own family circle and the bourgeois pastimes that were deemed appropriate for a woman of her class. The refined elegance captured in *At the Ball*, with the demurely averted glance of the young woman and the graceful gesture of the gloved hand that holds the fan, presents an image of cultivated and gracious womanhood, which would have been highly admired in the Morisot circles. The setting for the painting is the family home in the Rue Franklin, with the model placed in front of the same jardiniére that featured in an 1872 *Interior*. The title has more to do, therefore, with an atmosphere evoked through costume and pose, than the recording of an actual ball. The practice of dressing up models in formal or exotic costume was relatively common among Morisot's contemporaries and belies the assumption that the Impressionist painters cast a passive eye over an already existing world, which they then rendered objectively. The selection of scenes and the placing of models was crucial to the Impressionists, who evolved a technique designed to create the effect of impermanence and to approximate their own understanding of 'modernity'. In *At the Ball*, Morisot dressed her model in white, with white gloves and a pale fan, and placed her in a muted setting, relieved only by the brilliant touches of red, yellow and green in the flowers. The juxtaposition of white clothing and accessories with pale flesh enabled her to explore the colour of reflected light. The bluish and violet tonalities, with which Morisot so skilfully describes the shadows, had become, by this time, a hallmark of the Impressionist palette.

21
EVA GONZALÈS

A Loge at the Théâtre des Italiens
(c. 1874)

Oil on canvas
$38\frac{3}{4} \times 51\frac{1}{2}$ in. (98 × 130 cm.)
Musée d'Orsay, Galerie du Jeu de
Paume, Paris

When Gonzalès submitted this painting to the Salon in 1874 it was rejected by the jury and was only shown when she resubmitted it to the Salon of 1879. One critic, writing in 1874, claimed that Gonzalès's rejection was because of her connection with Manet, a Realist, and she declared: 'A realist is to painting what a radical is to politics'. In 1879 she was entered in the Salon catalogue as a pupil of Manet, and it was this association that prompted some negative response from critics. One of them declared that the bouquet in the bottom left-hand corner of the painting recalled the scandalous bouquet that Manet had included in his painting of a prostitute, *Olympia*, more than ten years previously. Manet had, in fact, never painted the well-dressed, genteel theatre audiences in their private boxes, which proved a popular subject for two of the women Impressionists. They found in it a modern life subject that fulfilled the current demand for paintings presenting the new urban reality of Third Republic France; further, it would not compromise their situation as bourgeois women for whom the activities of the *demi-monde*, so often painted by their male colleagues, would have been inaccessible. Gonzalès's painting not only reveals her commitment to representing modern life on a grand scale but also testifies to her awareness of contemporary painting techniques. The paint is vigorously applied in sweeping summary strokes. Critics expressed surprise that a painting by a woman could betray a vigour associated with 'masculinity', and which was widely thought to be derived from the work of Spanish artists like Velázquez, popular in Paris at the time.

As in *The Donkey Ride* (Plate 4), the woman occupies the central position, her gaze directed towards the viewer, with the man's body turned to face her. The figures appear almost theatrically illuminated, and the only indication that a world outside of the pictorial space might exist is provided by the woman's outward gaze and the pair of binoculars in her hand, which offers the promise of further vision.

22

MARY CASSATT

At the Opera
(1880)

Oil on canvas
32 × 26 in. (81 × 66 cm.)
Museum of Fine Arts (The Charles
Henry Hayden Fund), Boston

Cassatt painted at least eight variations of the theme of women at the opera, often placing her figures in front of a large mirror in which the theatre is reflected. In the painting *At the Opera*, it is the interaction between the principal model and the other figures that is central to the picture, so that no mirror is used in this composition. It was common in Paris in the late nineteenth century for women to dress elegantly for the opera, where they, almost as much as the performers, provided the spectacle. In Gonzalès's *A Loge at the Théâtre des Italiens* (Plate 21), the fashionably dressed woman holds her opera-glasses in her hand while her companion focuses his attention on her. In Renoir's *La Loge* (1874) the woman, elaborately costumed, again holds her opera-glasses, while her companion uses his to look across the opera house, perhaps at a party in another box. In Cassatt's painting, it is the woman who uses her glasses to stare intently across the theatre. She, simultaneously, is being scrutinized by a man who leans forward in an opposite box. In both the Gonzalès and Cassatt paintings, women are pictured as the object of a male look, a relationship that duplicates the habitual treatment of women as a spectacle. But the subject of Cassatt's painting is significantly woman as the bearer of the look. Her model is smartly but austerely dressed in black. Her fan is firmly clasped and shut, not alluringly posed as in Morisot's *At the Ball*, and her eyes are partially obscured by the opera-glasses through which she stares. Cassatt's woman is no object of seduction but commands the space in which she is placed. It is the scale of her framing silhouette against which all other forms in the painting are measured.

23
MARY CASSATT

Reading 'Le Figaro' (1878)

Oil on canvas
41 × 33 in. (104 × 84 cm.)
Private collection

At the end of 1877 Cassatt was joined in Paris by her parents, Robert and Katherine Cassatt, and her sister, Lydia. From this time on, her family was to become one of her major painting subjects.

The dignified woman pictured in *Reading 'Le Figaro'* is Cassatt's mother, Katherine Cassatt, who was exceptionally well educated and fluent in French, which she taught her children. It is appropriate, therefore, that Cassatt should represent her mother in an attitude of intense intellectual absorption. Katherine Cassatt was a regular reader of both French and American newspapers, and it was her intelligence and seriousness that provided an important role model for her daughter.

The imposing figure of Mrs Cassatt fills much of the canvas. The sobriety of the colour range and simple architectonic composition seem appropriate for this matter-of-fact, no-nonsense woman. Cassatt uses the opportunity to explore a wide range of muted grey, white and pale tonalities, now warming her whites with yellow, now cooling them with mauves and blue. Only the deep red of the pattern on the armchair provides a warm accent in the painting. The mirror reflection is confidently handled showing the grip of the hand on the newspaper, which is placed at the centre of the composition. It is to *Le Figaro* that Mrs Cassatt's gaze is directed; and it is to this object, with its obvious lettering, that the attention of the viewer is drawn. While images of women reading were very popular in the nineteenth century, few painters showed women reading newspapers, those documents of 'outside affairs' usually associated with men. In this image Cassatt presents the comfortable domain of the home, traditionally the sphere of women, here confidently reconciled through the image of her reading mother with the 'outside world', that of politics, business and intellect, symbolized by *Le Figaro*.

24
BERTHE MORISOT

Mother and Sister of the Artist
(1870)

Oil on canvas
$38\frac{1}{2} \times 32$ in. (100 × 81 cm.)
National Gallery of Art (Chester Dale
Collection), Washington, DC

Edma Pontillon, in white, is shown together with her mother in the family home in Paris, in the week preceding the birth of her first daughter.

The circumstances surrounding the creation of this painting reveal some of the insecurities felt by the young artist. Mme Morisot had written to Edma that the painter Puvis de Chavannes disliked the way that her head was painted. Edma responded supportively to her sister: 'I don't know what P. can have found wrong with the figure of mother; it seemed to me good.' Morisot had erased the head after Puvis's criticism. This was not to be the end of the painting's history, however. After telling Manet that she was feeling doubtful about the painting, Manet offered to advise her as to what needed to be done. In the event, he did much more than advise. Morisot wrote to her sister:

> He found it very good except for the lower part of the dress. He took the brushes and put in a few accents that looked very well; mother was in ecstasies. That is where my misfortunes began. Once started, nothing could stop him; from the skirt he went to the bust, from the bust to the head, from the head to the background. He cracked a thousand jokes, laughed like a madman, handed me the palette, took it back, finally by five o'clock in the afternoon we had made the prettiest caricature that was ever seen.

The work was accepted at the Salon. Both Morisot and her mother (who commented that Manet had spoiled the head) were angered at Manet's arrogance, yet afraid of offending him by withdrawing the painting. In the end, Morisot was not sorry that she had shown the work. She even submitted it, four years later, to the first Impressionist exhibition, thereby proving that she had recovered from the humiliation of Manet's intervention and was willing to acknowledge the painting as her own, despite his touches to the finished work.

25

BERTHE MORISOT

Portrait of Mme Pontillon (1871)

Pastel
32 × 25½ in. (81 × 65 cm.)
Musée du Louvre, Cabinet des Dessins,
Paris

Morisot's portrait of her sister was executed at the end of 1871 when Edma came to Passy for the birth of her second daughter. It was exhibited at the Salon of 1872 and shows Edma, pregnant and resigned with folded arms, on what seems to be the same comfortable floral sofa depicted in *The Mother and Sister of the Artist*, of the previous year. Morisot seems to have executed only two pastels before this highly skilled portrait, but from the early 1870s onwards, it became one of her favourite media and she is known to have executed nearly two hundred works in it. The family home, here depicted, was an important base for both Edma and Berthe.

Edma, herself, had been a promising painter and had shown in the Salons of 1864, 1865, 1867 and 1868. Her letters to Berthe after her marriage reveal how much she missed her sister and the artistic life they had shared. Berthe, in an attempt to comfort her sister after her marriage, had written: 'Men incline to believe that they fill all of one's life, but as for me, I think that no matter how much affection a woman has for her husband it is not easy to break with a life of work. Affection is a very fine thing, on condition that there is something else besides with which to fill one's days. This something I see for you in motherhood.' And in a comment that reveals her own frustrations added, 'Do not grieve about painting. I do not think it is worth a single regret.' Morisot represents her sister with a grandeur and dignity that is remarkable. The unmodulated blackness of the dress and shawl, with its beautifully captured transparency, which clothes the monumental figure of the pregnant woman, contrasts with the pale pink tinted flesh tones. The touching asymmetry of the face with the steady and penetrating gaze of the brown eyes indicate a model lovingly observed and sympathetically portrayed.

26

MARIE BRACQUEMOND

Lady in White (1880)

Oil on canvas
$71\frac{1}{2} \times 39\frac{1}{2}$ in. (181 × 100 cm.)
Musée de la Ville de Cambrai

This painting was first exhibited at the fifth Impressionist exhibition of 1880 and is one of a number of Bracquemond's paintings of single female figures in a garden. The subject was Louise Quiveron, Marie's sister, who was Marie's constant companion as well as her most frequent model. Bracquemond had, in 1877, painted *Woman in a Garden*, showing a fashionably dressed figure seated sideways on a chair, head turned to face the viewer, and it has been suggested that this could have been a study for the later painting. While it has been claimed that the *Lady in White* was executed *en plein air*, which the earlier painting clearly was not, the presence of preparatory drawings, notably a large, freely handled study in charcoal, reveals the careful consideration that Bracquemond gave to pictorial structure and composition. Indeed, the artist's son, has claimed that this was 'the last work executed by her in a classical technique'. His statement refers not only to the careful central placing of the figure, with the twisting of the torso to create the interest of a spiral arrangement, but to the still limited range of colour and careful modulation of tone. Bracquemond's submissions to the 1878 Universal Exhibition and the fourth Impressionist exhibition of 1879 had been large faience tile panels depicting the Muses of the Arts, which clearly demonstrated her skill in academic drawing and modelling. In *Lady in White*, however, although the linearity of this earlier style is evident, Bracquemond explores the effect of light on white fabric. Pierre Bracquemond claimed that 'white seen outdoors was a problem for study that excited the artist'. *Lady in White* is an important transitional work: while it retains a subtlety of colour derived from Corot and the Naturalists, and a clarity of outline from her classical training, it also shows the development of her exploration of colour and light. This was championed by the young *Independant* artists for whom she had a growing admiration.

27
MARY CASSATT

Little Girl in a Blue Armchair
(1878)

Oil on canvas
35 × 51 in. (89 × 130 cm.)
National Gallery of Art
(Collection of Mr and Mrs Paul Mellon),
Washington, DC

This painting is one of Cassatt's many images of childhood. The young girl is sprawled casually in a comfortable armchair, while a little lap-dog, of the type that Cassatt owned throughout her years in Paris, sleeps soundly in another. Although Cassatt had represented children before this, here we see a new element in her work, shown by the unselfconsciousness of the child and the exaggerated informality of the pose. She is presented as though unaware that she is being painted. The face, however, is still rendered in descriptive detail and the chairs are handled in an illustrative manner.

There is little sentimentality in this portrayal. The Salons of this period included many images of children with an overtly eroticized sweetness. Like Manet and Morisot in their paintings of children, so characterized by a detached and aloof restraint, Cassatt presents her subject in a matter-of-fact, coolly observed way.

The composition is asymmetrical, with all four edges appearing to have been cropped, and the central floor space seeming to tilt vertically. Cassatt's exploration of new compositional arrangements coincided with the start of her friendship with Degas, whom she met in 1877. He began to advise her on her work soon after. In a letter to the dealer Ambroise Vollard of 1903, she wrote of this painting:

I did it in 78 or 79—it was the portrait of a child of friends of Degas—I had done the child in an armchair, and he found that to be good and advised me on the background, he even worked on the background, I sent it to the American section of the Gd. exposition (of 1878) but it was refused. Since M. Degas had thought it good I was furious especially because he had worked on it—at that time it seemed new, and the jury consisted of three people, of which one was a pharmacist.

28

MARIE BRACQUEMOND

On the Terrace at Sèvres (1880)

Oil on canvas
34½ × 45 in. (88 × 115 cm.)
Musée du Petit Palais, Geneva

Some disagreement exists about the models for this painting. It was shown at the 1962 Bernheim Jeune retrospective of Bracquemond's work under the title *On the Terrace with M. Fantin-Latour, at Sèvres* and until recently was generally thought to represent Fantin-Latour and his wife Victoria Dubourg, with Marie Bracquemond to the left. It has been suggested, though, that the central figure cannot be identified as Fantin-Latour, a close friend of the family, as the model is clearly younger than the then forty-year-old artist. Pierre Bracquemond, in an unpublished manuscript, identifies both the female figures as his aunt, Louise Quiveron.

The painting was executed at the family home in the hills of Sèvres near Paris. It was first exhibited at the fifth Impressionist exhibition in 1880. Although painted in the same year as *Lady in White* (Plate 26), this painting and *The Three Graces* (Plate 10) reveal an artist who has absorbed the lessons of Impressionism. Gustave Geffroy in his *Histoire de l'Impressionnisme* connects Bracquemond's practice to that of the Impressionists by asserting that her painting follows 'the exact rules regulating the distribution of colour and its combination with light . . . Light is logically distorted, the colour ardently and harmoniously exalted . . . Three people rest in light-suffused shadow, the foliage immobile in the fiery atmosphere of the afternoon sun.'

Bracquemond, like her women colleagues, focuses most often on the figures in her compositions. Although the landscape is confidently handled, it provides no more than a background to the intimate group who form the subject of the painting. The finished painting is no spontaneous sketch. The artist's son recalled 'so many preparatory drawings, so many sketches before undertaking this canvas', and it is the combination of the monumentality of the figure grouping, so carefully arrived at, and the minute observations of qualities of light that give the painting its interest.

29
BERTHE MORISOT

The Cradle (1872)

Oil on canvas
$22\frac{1}{2} \times 18\frac{1}{2}$ in. (56×46 cm.)
Musée d'Orsay, Galerie du Jeu de
Paume, Paris

The Cradle represents Morisot's sister Edma with her daughter, born towards the end of 1871. It was shown at the first Impressionist exhibition of 1874. The critic Louis Leroy, in his satirical review of the exhibition, wrote:

> Now take Mlle Morisot! That young lady is not interested in reproducing trifling details. When she has a hand to paint, she makes exactly as many brushstrokes lengthwise as there are fingers, and the business is done. Stupid people who are finicky about the drawing of a hand don't understand a thing about impressionism, and great Manet would chase them out of his republic.

Although Manet himself did not show at the exhibition and tried in vain to persuade Morisot not to, the *Independant* artists were seen to be his disciples. Morisot's former teacher, Guichard, in reporting to her mother on the show declared: 'One doesn't live with impunity among madmen. Manet was right in opposing her participation.'

Morisot's small canvas shows her skill in using freely applied brushmarks to achieve the effect of transparency, her rejection of traditional tonal modelling and linear drawing, and her ability to capture the intimacy of an observed moment through painterly marks and a light palette, which was anathema to her academic critics.

The painting of mothers and children, with the mother's gaze often directed at the child, was one of the most popular subjects during the Third Republic. Motherhood was almost universally promoted as the only legitimate option for women, and paintings of mothers and children proliferated at the Salons of this time. Although Morisot's image can be said to evade some of the trappings of cloying sentimentality that characterized contemporary representations of this theme, it can nevertheless be viewed within this wider context.

In the autumn of 1880, Cassatt's brother Alexander and his family came to Paris, and it was during this visit that Cassatt executed the first of a number of portraits of the Cassatt children.

Mother about to Wash her Sleepy Child is her first *maternité* image, but already many of the elements of her later explorations of this theme are present. Most of the surface is filled with the monumental and enfolding presence of the mother in whose arms the infant is held. Her gaze is directed at the child, who sprawls in a typically ungainly childish fashion.

Many prototypes for such *maternité* images existed. Cassatt herself had studied the images of the 'Madonna and Child' by Correggio and Parmigianino and admired Rubens's paintings of this theme. The idea of investing motherhood with the sanctity and holiness associated with the Virgin Mary was common in nineteenth-century France. Mary, who had traditionally existed as a mystic intermediary, came to be seen as the Ideal Mother, the image of perfect womanhood, and a model for all women. The image of the 'modern madonna', that is a contemporary woman pictured in a composition with her child in a pose reminiscent of images of the Virgin and Child, became a very popular theme in visual representation in this period.

In her painting of 1880, the religious associations are tempered by the fact that the woman and infant have been closely observed from life. Painted at the height of Cassatt's involvement with 'realism' there is no doubt that this is a specific woman and her child pictured in the daily routine of washing. Nevertheless the associations of the pose remain strong, and for all its painterliness, accuracy of detail and simplicity of compositional design, the references to tradition remain strong.

31
BERTHE MORISOT

Eugène Manet and his Daughter in the Garden at Bougival (1881)

Oil on canvas
29 × 36 in. (73 × 92 cm.)
Private collection, Paris

Berthe Morisot, like Mary Cassatt, rarely used men as models. Her paintings of her husband, Eugène Manet (often including their daughter, Julie), executed on the Isle of Wight in 1875, at Bougival in 1881 and 1883 and in the garden at the rue de Villejust in 1886, are some of the few occasions when she does paint a man.

An amateur painter himself, Eugène Manet devoted much of his time to promoting his wife's work and organizing, with her, exhibitions of her paintings and those of her colleagues. He was her most ardent supporter and a sympathetic critic. The painting of Eugène Manet and his daughter are examples of the rare handling of the *paternité* theme. Manet is shown seated on a bench in the family garden, his attention focused on his three-year-old daughter, who is occupied with her game, which rests on his knee. The onus for educating daughters at this time was placed on mothers rather than fathers, and the theme of the 'mother educator' (*mère educatrice*) became an increasingly popular subject in painting and sculpture. It is interesting, therefore, that the sun-filled Bougival garden, with its well-cared-for flower beds and sumptuous colouring, is the setting for a scene of paternal devotion.

By the 1880s Morisot had abandoned all regard for academic standards of finish. Often working on a light brown ground, she painted directly and boldly, allowing the colour of the support to show through in places where only the barest marks indicate form and structure. As with *Young Woman Sewing in a Garden* (Plate 7), attention is drawn to the centre of the canvas, the edges and corners, at times, barely painted in. Her use of white in these images is boldly applied to the surface. Her palette is varied and contrasting, far removed now from the range of subtle and neutral tones of her early work.

32

MARY CASSATT

Alexander J. Cassatt and his Son, Robert Kelso Cassatt (1884)

Oil on canvas
39 × 32 in. (100 × 81 cm.)
Philadelphia Museum of Art
(The W.P. Wilstach Collection)

Cassatt's brother and his family paid regular visits to Paris from Philadelphia, which remained their home. Alexander Cassatt had become the first vice-president of the Pennsylvania Railroad and had accrued both power and wealth from this position, but in 1882 he resigned. Robert was one of four children of Alexander and Lois Buchanan-Cassatt who were some of Cassatt's favourite models. In the winter of 1884–5 she made a number of sketches of Robert, who proved to be a rather restless model. Cassatt's mother wrote to her granddaughter: 'Your Aunt Mary had a little thing of only two and a half years old to pose for her . . . She posed beautifully! I wish Robbie would do so half so well—I tell him that when he begins to paint from life himself, he will have a great remorse when he remembers how he teased his poor Aunt wriggling about like a flea.'

In a letter to his wife written toward the end of 1884, Alexander told her of the double portrait: 'Mary has commenced portraits of Robert and me together, Rob sitting on the arm of my chair . . . I don't mind the posing as I want to spend several hours a day with Mother anyhow and Rob will not have to pose much or long at a time.' Cassatt has placed her models so that their eyes are almost on the same level and the son looks like a miniature version of the father. The closeness of the pair is made apparent by the boy's arm with which he circles his father's shoulders. They are both dressed in black, and their flattened unmodulated torsos seem to merge. Unlike the Morisot *paternité* painting, where the father looks with indulgent concern at his daughter's game (Plate 31), this relationship is presented as one of emulation and identification. Alexander reads a book with the confident air of the patriarch, while the child seems to edge up to him, trying, as much as possible, to be like his father. It is that adult imperviousness and child's anxiety that this painting of a father and son relationship so admirably captures.

GENERAL BOOKS FOR FURTHER REFERENCE

ANNE SUTHERLAND HARRIS and LINDA NOCHLIN *Women Artists 1550–1950* Los Angeles, 1978.

ROZSIKA PARKER and GRISELDA POLLOCK *Old Mistresses: Women, Art and Ideology* London, 1981.

LINDA NOCHLIN 'Why Have There Been No Great Women Artists?', *Art and Sexual Politics* (eds. Bauer and Hess), New York and London, 1973.

CLAUDE ROGER MARX 'Les femmes peintres et l'impressionnisme', *Gazette des Beaux-Arts* vol 38, Paris, 1907.

The Journal of Marie Bashkirtseff new edition (introd. by Roszika Parker and Griselda Pollock), London, 1985.

THEODOR DE WYZEWA *Peintres de jadis et d'aujourd'hui* Paris, 1903.

CHARLOTTE YELDHAM *Women Artists in Nineteenth-Century England and France* New York and London, 1984

JEAN-PAUL BOUILLON, ELIZABETH KANE 'Marie Bracquemond', *Woman's Art Journal* Fall 1984/Winter 1985

NANCY MOWLL MATHEWS (ed.) *Cassatt and her Circle* New York, 1984.

GRISELDA POLLOCK *Mary Cassatt*, London, 1980.

ADELYN BREESKIN *Mary Cassatt, A Catalogue Raisonné of Paintings, Watercolours and Drawings* Washington, 1970

JOHN BULLARD *Mary Cassatt, Oils and Pastels* New York and Oxford, 1972.

CLAUDE ROGER MARX *Eva Gonzalès* Paris, 1950.

DENIS ROUART (ed.) *The Correspondence of Berthe Morisot* New York, 1959; republished and edited by Tamar Garb and Kathleen Adler, London, 1986.

MONIQUE ANGLOUVENT *Berthe Morisot* Paris, 1933.

KATHLEEN ADLER, TAMAR GARB *Berthe Morisot* London, forthcoming.

M. L. BATAILLE, G. WILDENSTEIN *Catalogue Raisonné of the Oil Paintings, Pastels and Watercolours of Berthe Morisot* Paris, 1961.

ELIZABETH KANE 'The Artist Time Forgot', *Apollo* February 1983.

ACKNOWLEDGEMENTS

Many people have helped, both directly and indirectly, in the writing of this book. It is, above all, the product of the integration of my involvement with academic art history with my experiences in the women's movement. It was through my experiences at the Women's Therapy Centre that I was, through a slow process of learning and sharing, able to stand outside the traditional boundaries of art history to ask new questions about women's role in the making of art and in the way that women's contribution to art has been produced through art history. Without the framework of the centre and the strength provided by the women with whom I shared so much, I could not have been in a position to write this book.

To Kathy Adler for her patience and care in reading a number of half completed drafts and to Rasaad Jamie for his searching comments and tireless willingness to listen, I am deeply grateful. I am indebted too to John House for his continued support and helpful comments and to Lorna Taylor and Yves Couder, whose generosity in opening their beautiful Paris home to me made doing the research for this book a pleasure.   TAMAR GARB

The publishers wish to thank all private owners, museums, galleries, libraries and other institutions for permission to reproduce works in their collections. Further acknowledgement is made for the following illustrations:
11, 22: Courtesy Museum of Fine Arts, Boston: fig. 6: reproduced by Courtesy of the Trustees of the British Museum; 19: L. L. Coburn Fund Income, © The Art Institute of Chicago, all rights reserved; front cover, 23:

© Christie's Colour Library; fig. 2: Charles W. Harkness Fund, The Cleveland Museum of Art; 1, 13, 16, 21, 29, figs. 1, 5: Cliché des Musées Nationaux, Paris; 20, 31, back cover: Lauros-Giraudon, Paris; 9: The Metropolitan Museum of Art, New York, all rights reserved; 6: Photo Bulloz, Paris; 14: Photo, Ray Delvert, Villeneuve-sur-Lot; 5: Gift of Mr and Mrs Abraham Sonnabend, Brookline, Massachusetts. Ektachrome, Muldoon Studio, Waltham, Massachusetts.